Nature's Whispers

Faith Whatley-Blaine

BookLeaf
Publishing

India | USA | UK

Presentation by *BookLeaf Publishing*

Web: www.bookleafpub.com

E-mail: info@bookleafpub.com

ISBN: 9789363310100

First edition 2024

*To those who believed, supported, and loved
me. Life and my accomplishments would mean
nothing without all of you.*

PREFACE

My love of nature started in a creek when I was younger. My mom, dad, sister, and I would play for hours chasing dragonflies, naming turtles, and creating memories. This instilled in me a profound desire to be in nature and led me to become a competitive rock climbers, hiker, and typical adventurer.

My real journey to nature started right around the time of Covid. As I was kicked out of my dorm, forced into a digital learning environment and unable to work due to the outbreak, I felt more alone than ever before. The lack of human connection led me to look for connection to something else. When all else left me, nature was there to catch me. My family took a cross-country trip passing through the beautiful canyons of Utah to visit the sights of California. From Joshua Tree to Rocky Mountains, I found an environment where I could feel so wonderfully insignificant in the world and be okay with that. I found solace in all aspects of nature from storms, trees, the ocean, and everything in between.

This chapbook lives as a physical manifestation of my experiences with nature and the lessons it has taught me over the past years. I hope you enjoy this collection and wish you luck and happiness in your next adventure!

As It Begins

It's how every reckless adventure begins, isn't
it?

With a certain restlessness nestled
In the heart of an unwearied traveler
An unrelenting itch that can only be scratched
by
A sea salt infused breeze or fresh pine mixed
with firesmoke

Some perceive these individuals as extremists
Desperate to run away from something
Perhaps responsibilities, decisions, society

Hibernating on the outskirts of the world
Hiding from the harsh realities of life

But I dissent

I believe those who see life in Earth's shadows
And have 'wanderlust' carved onto their ribcage

The astrophiles, the ecopoets, the radicals
Who decipher stars
And pray to Mother Nature

Are racing towards something
Chasing sunlight and morning dew
That addictive feeling of being alive

So, with one part reckless and
Two parts abandonment
We throw on our muddy boots
Grab our keys and our courage
Then set our next destination to

'Anywhere but here'

Just as every great adventure begins.

Her Symphony

I travel to bare witness to
Her soul soothing melodies
Her madrigals that ebb and flow
Following the direction of the moon

She whispers notes to
Guide her unwitting musicians
Hands dripping with passion
Shaping an inimitable aria

The whistling wind seasoned with sea salt
Paired perfectly with scrappy young love
Which can never keep a consistent tempo

She prompts the percussionists for
Splashing statticos of seagull squawks,
Warning cymbals from lifeguard whistles, and
Arpeggios of laugher with an accent of childlike
wonder

If you listen close enough you can discern
A medley of college friends' inside jokes
Duetted with flashes from cameras,
A futile attempt to duplicate unduplicable
moments

Followed by a slight diminuendo signaled by
Parents calling children for home,
The decrescendo of tourist chatter, and
Sandcastles demolished by the incoming tide

I remain until the buskers strike their final chord
Until the lovers drift to motionlessness
Until all that remains is Her

She turns with a Mona Lisa expression
Framed by her reflective, turquoise hair
Presents an appreciate nod, before beginning
again

The audience may leave before her final bow

But I stay

How could I tear myself away?

Persistence

A single daisy

Born under asphalt

Little sunlight

Little water

All alone

Destined to die

Yet, she didn't

Forced herself out

Clawing to light

Thirsting for rain

Cultivating love

Against all

She bloomed

Western Wisconsin

We dared down
The winding path

Paved with curiosity
Imparted by those
Who ambled before us

Our minds could not fathom
How Heaven escaped
To Earth, beaming through
The cracks of the branches

Nor how the display of
Sepia tinted leaves
Created a sunset below
The Hickory trees

This scene either
Escaped from grandma's
Fingerprint-stained storybook or
Midas previously roamed
This trail creating an aureate
Forest in his footsteps

No other explanation is plausible

Glimpse: I

crackling light
interrupts the
blurry darkness,
revealing potholes
with rippling puddles,
content holding
the Universe's
infinite reflection

The Cliffside

An anachronistic Cycad plead
His case for permission to fall

Rooted in the Purgatory
Of charcoal skies
And dirty crashing waves

His cataphylls fall, victim
To the brutish wind

The luring waves taunted
The holy skies judged
The persistent gales pushed

His tattered soul which
Raged against the tide
That sought his demise

Until there was
No resist left

Against the weight of the sky
He could no longer endure

So, another tree fell

Without a witness around

Legend has it,
He left his pleading heart
On that ledge still
Searching for a reason

As a warning to those
Who trespass into hopelessness

Daring them to turn back
Before the only way out
Is down

Winter's Beginning

Only echoes of loss remain;
Barren saplings stripped of life;
A once technicolor landscape;
Forced into grayscale;
In the frigid quiet, grief settles;
Blanketing the world in a silent shroud;
Snowflakes drift like gentle tears;
Finding companionship in winter's bite;
Nature's harsh reminder;
That all we cherish;
Will one day die.

Cloudgazing

I sit beneath the boundless azul canvas;

Lost in this fluid tapestry;

Careless cotton candy clouds drift by;

Each one painting a new portrait;

I lay transfixed by these shapeless forms;

With affectionate melodies in my ear;

Our first dance emerges like a movie in the sky;

In this timeless moment I linger;

Until reality gently reclaims me;

My scene disappears with the changing wind;

Reminding me this fleeting beauty;

Will remain merely a passing moment.

Creek Memories

Beneath the pine's watchful canopy;
Little toes dance in a babbling current;
Chasing shadows of darting minnows;
Stirring water scorpions;
Eliciting playful screams;
Childhood memories tickle my mind;
Recalling skipping stones across our reflections;
Laughter echoing through the sun-dappled
grove;
Muddy hands crafting miniature dams;
Imagination roaming wild and free;
As the creek murmurs secrets to eager ears;
These memories remain etched into my soul.

Directions

1. Once you pass the rusted traffic light sporadically flashing red, take a left at the first bluejay
2. Then turn the opposite direction of the last house you see
3. Continue until the sky is at your fingertips, then turn right
4. Go straight until you spy a rabbit or deer. If you spot a rabbit first, remember your first kiss and then continue straight. If you see a deer first, turn left
5. Drive until the road ends
6. Adorn your muddy hiking books and start on the trail lined with pine needles and fallen acorns
7. Take the first right
8. After two minutes and thirty-two seconds, turn towards the quietest part of the forest and continue forward
9. Once you see seven squirrels you will come to a fork in the road, take the beaten middle path
10. If you don't see the path in the middle, go back to step six and try again
11. Continue straight until you begin to question your place in the world, then take a left

12. Walk until you start to get a tingly feeling
that travels from your fingertips to your toes
13. Breathe that aliveness in until it consumers
you, until you are so overwhelmed you want to
cry (it's okay if you do, I did too)
14. Remain in that moment until you finally
understand the meaning of it all
15. Then breathe that feeling back out, you must
leave it here for the next wanderer

Glimpse: II

sunbeams
glare against
the soft waves,
a mirror lapping
against the golden
sand, hiding
the Ocean's
treasured secrets

Stardust

Born from stardust;
Your atoms are celestial heirlooms;
The cosmos dance in your veins;
Worlds collided to create you;
Molecules of miracles;
How dare you doubt your worth?

Humbling

With crackling flames and illuminated faces;
We gather under ancient dreams with;
Smoke and tranquility swirling in the wind;

An avowed stargazer, I cast my eyes;
Heavenwards, plotting the;
Imaginary lines traced by apophenia.

Asteroids, planets, and stars;
Scattered across the velvet sky;
Beacons of untold stories;

A gentle reminder of our place;
Insignificant amidst and humbled by;
The vastness of this universe.

Autumn's Lesson

What blossomed with kisses by a lake teeming
with koi turned barren by early dusk;

My bereft love now rests neglected, lost
somewhere between misunderstanding and
apathy;

So I passed with the leaves creating a crimson
carpet on the forest floor;

And turned to Autumn to teach me how to let go
of what needed to die.

1am Conversations

She and I, kindred spirits,

Solitary travelers in the cosmos,

Yet constant companions to steadfast stars,

She finds solace in the silence,

As do I.

Renowned for mirroring not creating,

Phasing through aesthetics,

Shining brightest in the quiet hours.

When insomnia haunts me,

We converse.

She laments how inertia ensnared her,

Forever destined to orbit another's path,

Forbidden from drawing near

Condemned to live vicariously,

I empathize.

Though I may never fathom the her plight,

I listen, captivated by how such beauty feels
confined,

How brilliance can be so estranged,

Perhaps, she wonders the same of me.

Winter's Ending

Amidst the frigid quiet,
An abandoned candle flickers;
Slowing thawing grief into hope;
Underneath depression's blanket;
Our dormant dreams still lie;
In the crisp air, nature whispers gently;
Promises of resilience and renewal;
So I wait with this belief:
With each moonrise;
The sun draws nearer;
To shining once again.

Her Choice

She swayed on the threshold between two
worlds
One dark one light her past and her future
Tulip petals fell from her fingertips
Bringing color to the dead grass beneath
Her bare feet which have never known the dark
If you were to look close enough you'd see
Pomegranate seeds and adventure caught
In the gaps of her teeth as she grinned
Stepping towards the loving darkness before her

Glimpse: III

summits kiss the
spotless azure sky
with bleached snow
overlapping dark
conifers, plotting
out the path to the
peak of the Mountain's
breathtaking wonders

My Sister

Some say she was born with spring in her blood;

Always donning a bright smile reflecting her
disposition;

You would recognize her if you saw her;

With cherry blossoms and sunshine woven into
her chestnut curls;

A small monarch tattoo on her left wrist and rose
petal lips;

Her infectious laughter dances among
dogwoods;

Seeping into the ears of those blessed to
encounter her;

She is an illustration of how to rebloom after
winter;

How to live after darkness consumes everything;

With spring coursing through her veins she
promenades;

Leaving daffodils and new beginnings in her
footsteps.

Wash Me Away

Her anger is at my doorstep again,
   Relentlessly raging against the frosted panes
    Flashes foreshadowing her subsequent
screams;

I try to ignore it, I promise,
   But her magnetic pull is
    Too strong for my cobalt heart.

Perhaps I am just too desperate
   To be seen, known, understood,
    By someone with my same fury;

I race out to rebel against all that is holy,
   Stumbling into the Sky's tears surrendering
    To my knees, begging her to Wash me
Away

She obliged and saturated my soul
   Reviving me in her divine downpour
    Baptizing me in her Mother's name

Amidst the chaos of her wrath
   I found part of myself previously
    Stolen by the cruelty of the world;

The Sky and I then sat together,
    In distorted silence and understanding
        Until the last raindrop touched Earth

I slowly picked up
    The pieces of myself
        Gave the Sky a kiss, then left

I pray that someday, you too
    Will know the experience of
        Screaming at the Sky
            And for her to bellow back

Learning to Listen

they whispered
softly in silence

breathed of the
universe's secrets;

hidden in the cracks
of everydayness.

for a pure moment
finally, i understood.

i cannot tell you
what they said;

for that is between
me and the leaves.